Finish a Fi ONE move

Without Any Training

'The Martial Arts for Beginners Series'

By Justyn Billingham

Dedicated to anyone that likes to venture outdoors every now and again

Disclaimer
Please note that the author of this book is not responsible in any manner whatsoever for any damage or injury of any kind that may result from practicing, or applying , the principles, ideas, techniques and/or following the instructions/information described in this book. Since the physical activities in this book may be to strenuous in nature for some readers to engage in safely, it is essential that a doctor be consulted before undertaking training.

Table of Contents

Introduction

There are only TWO guarantees in life.

One, we're all going to die.

And two, if you arrange to have friends over for a BBQ during the height of British Summer Time… it will rain.

Just because you have the fastest car it doesn't mean you're going to finish first.

Just because you have the best team, it doesn't mean you're going to win the match.

All these things should make a difference.

But there's always that possibility that they don't.

Nothing's certain.

NOTHING!

And so it is with self defence.

You see, I have spent the past thirty years studying many different types of fighting systems to a very high level.

I have been on many a self defence / protection / workshop / seminar / course.

I have been on many a knife defence workshop / seminar / course.

I have read many self defence / protection books.

I have watched many self defence / protection videos.

I have watched hours and hours of CCTV footage of street fights and street attacks.

I have witnessed street fights and street attacks first hand.

I have seen people get sprayed in the eyes with mace (or similar) and still overpower the person that sprayed them.

I have seen people get tasered and it have little to no effect on them.

I have seen people get stabbed and still keep fighting, some not even realising they've actually been stabbed.

I have seen people get shot, several times, at relatively close range and still manage to keep on fighting.

I have worked as a doorman.

I have worked in security.

I have trained and learnt from the very best in the world.

I have fought competitively to a very high level in competition.

And I have been on the receiving end of violence myself.

And one thing I can tell you for certain is that nothing (**NOTHING!**) is a **GUARANTEE** when it comes to fighting or defending yourself.

And this is **VERY** important for you to understand because I want to make it completely clear that regardless of how much money you pay to attend a seminar / workshop or self defence type course.

Regardless of what the cover of a book **PROMISES** you.

Regardless of how much the person teaching you *is* an **EXPERT** in their field.

There is no move or technique that anyone can absolutely **GUARANTEE** will finish a fight or attack instantly.

And that's the key word in all of this….

GUARANTEE.

Nothing at all is a guarantee in life (except that you're going to die… oh, and the BBQ thing).

And there is no real secret to defending yourself.

It's not some magical, mystical, spiritual thing that only certain people know about.

It really is just a case of common sense.

A little know how (which I'm going to share with you).

And a little understanding of the human body.

So before we continue.

Or rather (if you're reading this using the '*Look Inside*' option, before you part with any of your hard earned money (and do note that I'm not asking you to spend any more on this… my life's work, than you would on a pint of beer, a glass of wine or a bar of chocolate), then you need to know that I think I already know the kind of person you are.

I think you're the kind of person that probably doesn't want to spend most of their evenings breaking a sweat and pushing your body through all those limits all while someone shouts and screams clichés at you.

You just want to know that if you felt your life was ever in danger, you could deal with the situation.

Because that's all I actually ever wanted.

And I don't believe I'm any different to you.

You'll read about my very first street encounter in the next chapter.

It's the reason I started studying the fighting arts.

I've devoted over thirty years of my life to those fighting arts.

And I won't lie, I hated it at first.

I would have happily quit a million times over.

What kept me going was the fear of being attacked again.

So while my mates were all out on a weekend terrorizing the neighbourhood as teenagers often do.

Or trying their hardest to get served their first under age pint in our local pub.

I was working in a hot sweaty pub kitchen, washing pots and pans at aged fourteen just so that I could pay for my own training, as my mother couldn't afford to.

And although my training has become a way of life now, the fact that *you're* looking through this book indicates that you've either been attacked.

Or you're *concerned* about being attacked.

And you're hoping to find something in one of the many *'self defence'* style books out there that will put your mind at rest.

So let me try.

Everything I talk about in this book is based on my own firsthand experience.

And everything I talk about in this book has worked… for me.

And it *can* work for you without you needing to devote thirty years of your life to it.

You don't even need to join an expensive gym or martial art school.

I *will* suggest a few *simple* things that you can have a bit of fun with later and will help you to determine your best weapons but overall I want to show you how you *can* walk away unscathed from a street encounter without ever having set foot on a self defence seminar.

As ultimately that's what I believe *'self defence'* is really all about.

And if that offers you any reassurance at all you still need to know one key thing.

Either EVERYTHING works or NOTHING works.

It's all purely down to circumstances.

But please don't *ever* let ANYONE tell you that any of this is a GUARANTEE.

Because it's not.

And putting your trust in someone to that degree and believing it is.

Could get you seriously hurt.

Or even killed.

My Very First Street Attack

"Do you fancy joining me and my dad on a trip to France?"

I'd never been to France.

Never actually been abroad at that point in my life to be honest.

I'd had the occasional week's holiday to Fairbourne in Wales when I was growing up, but only with the grandparents (on my mother's side) as my mother couldn't afford to take us away anywhere on her own.

And I loved Fairbourne as a young kid.

Those great times I'd share with the family sheltering under an umbrella on the beach in the rain.

Paddling in the freezing cold sea.

Eating over priced and stone cold hot dogs made up from bits of animal that clearly wasn't meat.

Priceless childhood memories!

I was the older of two kids in a single parent family, and it was back in the 70's when things were a bit different to how they are today.

It was more of a given back then (at least in the industrial town where I grew up) that the father went out to work and the mother stayed at home, and so when my father walked out on us all, all we had to sustain us was the state benefit handouts and the (very) little amount of money he was forced (by the courts), to provide my mother with so she could clothe, feed, and wash us all while trying to keep a roof over our heads.

So needless to say at fourteen years old, and with no way of funding it myself, and combined with the fact that my mother was a rather overly protective kind of parent, I really didn't think I would be allowed to go to France at all.

But luckily for me my mate's dad, who was a proper bloke as I remember, the kind of man that spent all his time either working in the factory or getting drunk in the pub with all his rough neck mates, had a chat with my mother and convinced her that as he and his thirty odd mates were simply hiring the fifty two seater coach to head over to Boulogne in France, load it up with cheap hypermarket beer and then turn straight back round again and head back to Blightly -- not even bothering to actually venture into France, nothing could possible happen to me.

So she agreed I could go!

And he was right.

I mean, after all, what could possibly go wrong???

So we arrived in Boulogne at whatever time it was and myself and my seven other mates were told to 'sod off and meet back here in a few hours' so we did.

At least that was the plan.

We'd have a little wonder around, see the amazing sights of Boulogne and then jump straight back onto the coach and endure the twenty hour journey back to the UK.

Great fun!

Now I remember it very well.

After about ten minutes of not having a clue where we were heading we arrived at a very busy main road.

I think there was something like six lanes to this highway and we needed to cross them but as the traffic was so busy we all just carried on walking parallel to it waiting for a break in the traffic so we could cross.

And a small break did appeared so I, and two more of my friends, seized the opportunity to play chicken with some French cars and made a bolt for it, arriving safely on the other side much to the dismay of our other four friends who remained on the original side of the street like a bunch of suckers.

One nil to us!

So we all continued heading towards the town centre, maintaining the same route and staying parallel to the main road in the hope that another break in the traffic would soon present itself and the four losers on the other side of the road could catch up with us once more.

And I felt a tap on the shoulder.

Now I was walking on the outside of our little trio, nearest to the road and you know when one of your mates does that hilarious thing where they lean over your far shoulder and tap you on it so you look the other way and then everyone laughs at you because you fell for it like an idiot… well that's what I thought was going on.

So I ignored him.

And then he tapped me on the shoulder again.

But being the smart kind of streetwise kid I was I figured I'd turn the tables on him and look in his general direction instead ruining his little attempt at pranking me and making him the fool… which is when I spotted the two rather large chaps walking very close behind us.

Now they both smiled and in broken English engaged me in conversation which went something like this….

Them -- "Alright?"

Me -- "Yes thanks!"

Them -- "You English?"

Me -- "Yeah."

Them -- "What you doing here?"

And all the time both of them wearing a very welcoming smile and putting me completely at ease and, as I now understand the psychology of a street attack so much better, drawing me in and subconsciously lowering my defences.

Me -- "Umm, we're just here for the day having a look round."

Them -- "That's nice." Big smiles all round from both of them. "You got any money?"

Me -- "Err, yeah."

Them -- "You give it to us"

Now at this point in the conversation I realised something wasn't quite right.

They still maintained their conversational tone but I could tell that the actual words they were now using didn't quite match up to the way they were saying them.

And I found this quite confusing.

And at this stage I should perhaps mention that although I'd spent my fourteen years to date living in a bit of a rough old part of town, I'd never been in a situation where I'd felt threatened in any way.

Certainly not the *'I'm in a foreign country, can't speak the language, haven't got a clue where I am and the only adults that might be able to bring this to a stop were some distance away loading up their hypermarket trolley's with crates of cheap beer... oh, and there was no such thing as mobile phones back then either'* kind of threatened.

So a little unsure of what was actually happening to me and in turn where this was actually leading I just said, with a frown and a slight disdainful tone...

"No!"

So he punched me -- full force in the face.

I'd never been punched in the face before.

I made out to all my mates that I was a bit of a scrapper because that got you a bit of street cred and respect, but to be honest it was just lies.

I think I may have staggered backwards a bit -- I can't quite remember if I'm being honest, but as soon as his punch connected with my cheek bone my body dumped a whole load of adrenaline, as it does, to give me the strength and energy to fight back or run away (fight or flight) and as most victims do... I just froze.

Rooted to the spot and *'frozen with fear'* -- as the cliché goes.

My legs felt like they had suddenly turned into jelly.

My heart raced so fast I thought it might actually explode.

But rather bizarrely I didn't actually feel the pain of the punch… which I now know is because the combination of shock and adrenaline had simply anesthetised the pain.

Instead I just stared back at him, with wide open disbelieving eyes unable to move, react or even speak.

And for a very brief moment I saw a look of surprise in my assailants eyes as I think he was expecting that punch to have had somewhat of a different effect.

I'd never been punched in the face before so instead of dropping to my knees screaming in pain, running away or fighting back… I just stood there, emotionless staring right back at my attacker, because to be honest, I didn't know what else to do.

And I think this strange reaction momentarily surprised him.

"I ask again, you give us money."

Now at this point I suddenly realised something else was wrong.

My two mates that had been there at the start of all of this were suddenly no longer next to me.

In fact they were nowhere to be seen at all.

But that's okay I thought as there are actually seven of us and just two of them so when the rest of my mates get across that bloody road these two Frenchies will be in for one hell of a shock.

Especially as all my mates are supposedly good fighters -- so they keep telling everyone!

"I don't have any money!"

THUD -- he punched me again, right in the same spot.

I stared back at him, my heart racing inside my body still.

Adrenaline pumping through my veins.

Unable to move.

I couldn't even lift my hands in a feeble attempt to half heartedly try and defend myself.

Plus, I didn't really know what to do with them even if I could have lifted them up.

I just stood there staring at him as he punched me in the face again.

At this point his mate, who had stayed silent throughout, reached a hand into his inside jacket pocket and said something in French to my attacker.

My attacker put his hand out to stop his mate from pulling out whatever it was he had hidden in that pocket and shook his head.

A knife!

He's got a knife and he's going to stab me with it and if he does I might die.

Now when those thoughts go through your mind at any stage in your life I think they must stay with you forever.

Mine certainly have.

When you literally see your life flash before your very eyes it has a lasting effect on you.

My attacker then grabbed me by the collars of my jacket and holding me firmly in place with his outstretched arms said "I ask again… you give me money!"

Well at that point, and with great hindsight, I now realise that I should have just given it to him.

It wasn't much in all fairness and certainly not worth dying for but in my defence I genuinely thought that if I now give him my money he'll realise I've been lying to him all along and so not only will he take my money but he'll then stab me for lying… so in my head I thought I'd better try and maintain the lie.

"I told you, I don't have any money!"

And that's when he head butted me, right on the nose splitting it right open.

Yet true to form, and despite the fact that if at that point I'd have been offered a mirror I'd have seen that my face probably looked quite a state by now, I just simply stared back at him -- terrified.

So he grabbed me with his left hand by the scruff of my neck and with his right hand raised three fingers in the air.

Where the hell are my mates I thought?

"Last chance, three…"

He lowered his thumb leaving two fingers hanging in the air.

"Two…"

He lowered his middle finger leaving just one finger hanging in the air.

All the time I was just staring him right in the eyes, not even able to cringe at what was surely about to come my way.

"One!"

He lowered his final finger making a perfect fist and, while still holding me in place and therefore keeping me from cowering away, used it to punch me repeatedly in the face only finally stopping after landing several heavy blows and turning to his mate, who still had his hand inside his jacket, said....

"NOW!"

Well thankfully for me I didn't get knifed that day.

Instead and oh, the irony of it... I got hit full force in the face with some kind of anti-mugging spray.

But I thought they'd thrown acid in my face.

I don't know exactly what it was they used on me but whatever it was it burned like hell.

I was blinded.

My eyes streamed.

My nose ran.

And the skin on my face felt like it was on fire.

I dropped to my knees, holding my face and screamed out as loud and for as long as I could.

Within about five seconds I heard a familiar voice....

"Don't worry mate, we got ya."

It was my two friends who, along with the other four, had watched the whole thing unfold from a safe little distance away.

Well they managed to kind of frog walk me back to the coach, chuck me in the back while someone went in to inform the dads as to what had happened.

And in their defence, once the dads had fully stocked the coach with their cheap beer and had a bite to eat they agreed that the best thing to do was for us all to head back to the UK and I could go to hospital there instead as no one wanted to be stuck in Boulogne any longer than they had to be -- which I thought was really kind of them.

So thankfully the effect of that spray only lasted about 24 hours.

My eyesight returned to normal, although I did have to travel back to the UK unable to open my eyes at all and having to enduring masses of pain.

But the best thing (and I'm being very sarcastic here) was that over a period of about a week, all the skin peeled off my face leaving me looking like some kind of leper, much to the amusement of EVERYONE in my high school and as kids will be kids (especially teenage kids) I became the butt of all the jokes for some considerable time afterwards.

In fact if I ever bump into someone from my class at school I still get reminded of the many nicknames I got branded with… some thirty years on!

But on reflection the one thing that stood out for me the most, and I have told this story many, many times before, was that despite being out in France with six of my mates.

And despite people walking past.

Adults.

Parents.

And all of them having a good old look.

No one.

Not one person.

Did anything to help me.

They all left me to deal with the beating by myself.

Because unfortunately, and I hate to say it, but it's true....

No one actually wants to get involved, step in or help out in a situation like this, just in case the attacker(s) turn on them and they themselves end up getting hurt.

And I do understand this as it stems from that self preservation gene that we all have.

And of course it's human nature.

How many times have you stopped to help someone that's broken down at the side of the road?

But know that although there may be a few 'good Samaritans' out there that *may* jump in to save you.

Or you may be out with your mates.

Or your partner.

Do not ever solely bank on the fact that someone will step in to help you.

The vast majority of the time you are probably going to have to deal with a street attack on your own so prepare for that.

And you're certainly going to have to deal with a fight on your own.

....

A week later I enrolled into my very first martial arts class!

Fight Or Flight?

In the last chapter I briefly mentioned something called 'Fight or Flight'.

The Fight or Flight response is a recognised reaction that occurs when we suddenly find ourselves in a dangerous, harmful or life threatening situation.

It is supposed to be a good thing and is there to help us deal with any situation in which we may need additional strength, speed, stamina, energy or pain tolerance.

We've all heard those incredible stories of the mothers that lift up those cars that mow down their children.

Or the soldiers walking several miles to safety on two broken legs.

Adrenaline normally has something to do with those amazing feats of superhuman endurance that we often get to hear about.

However this natural inbuilt *'thing'* that is biologically designed to help us save our own lives… can sometimes also be our downfall.

So let's gain a greater understanding of adrenaline and how it works and why it might not always be such a great thing to have after all.

Believe it or not, we're not actually at the top of the food chain.

I know we're led to believe we are but the truth is… if we take away all of our walls and guns, we're not.

I recently went on a safari holiday where I got to spend five of the most incredible days up close and personal (and very safe in the jeep) with some of the most amazing animals I've ever seen without there being a big fence in between both of us.

And after a couple of days and having asked the same question over and over to my poor, unassuming tracker, 'what would *that* do if I got out of the jeep now?' one thing became quite obvious to me....

All of those animals, even the 'prey' ones (y'know, the ones that are really only there to get eaten), even they are naturally bigger, faster or stronger (or all three) than us mere human beings.

And all of them come readily armed with their own natural 'weapons'.

Even the prey ones have huge great spiky things protruding from their head which if they caught you with would do massive amounts of damage... possibly even kill you.

Us... well we can throw our fists about a bit.

Maybe even try kicking.

I remember one of my old school martial art instructors even telling me that one of his spinning back kicks would drop a charging rhino.

That I would have loved to see for real!

And we'd have to get really close (too close) to be able to do any real damage with our pathetic little teeth.

I watched a couple of lionesses hunting down a pack of wildebeest on about day three.

The way these two lionesses stalked their prey was incredibly impressive.

One lioness went down one side of the herd and the other lioness went down the other and it was as if they were somehow communicating to one another telepathically.

And yet somehow the Wildebeest knew they were there.

Unusually not one was moving and all stood incredible still facing in the general direction of their attackers.

I don't know if they *could* actually see these two lionesses but, faced with certain danger and very possibly death for one of them, they *all* stood their ground.

And yet this didn't put off either of these two lionesses who very stealthily under cover of the long grass, stalked ever closer.

And then, after about thirty minutes of ever so carefully closing the gap between them and their next meal, when she thought she was close enough, one of the lioness went for it, sprinting for all she was worth.

But it was badly timed as every single one of those Wildebeest took off as fast as they could -- a real life stampede, and quite incredible to witness.

And so that was that -- foiled.

And that got me thinking.

We, mere human beings, are no different from those animals really.

We all function in the same way.

So why, when faced with a life threatening situation did those Wildebeest all take to their heels, run for the hills away from danger and all live to see yet another day when you hear time and time again that when a human being is faced with a life threatening situation… we freeze?

I did it myself as you've just read about.

Well I'll tell you.

It's because as human beings we've become domesticated.

We've had every conceivable law passed in order to keep us safe.

When we leave home each morning it's pretty much a given that we will return home again that same evening.

But not for those Wildebeest.

They leave home every morning with a massively high chance that one of them won't return.

That one of them will get attacked, killed and eaten.

So what's a Wildebeest got to do with me learning that one move death punch you promised to teach me which is the only reason I bought this book, I hear you ask?

Well I'll tell you.

You see in the days of the caveman, when we had to go out hunting and gathering, there's was a huge risk that as pretty much everything out there was bigger than us (as it still is) we might not actually make it back again.

And so as it was quite likely that we'd turn a corner and come face to face with a hungry sabre toothed tiger, our bodies would dump a whole load of adrenaline into our bloodstream and we would use this sudden surge of energy, speed, power and strength to run away as fast as our little legs would carry us.

Or, if we couldn't run away, we could then stand and fight.

Just like those Wildebeest.

And we'd unfortunately face this *'we might just get killed and eaten today'* risk on a daily basis.

So we'd be used to dealing with huge rushes of adrenaline pumping through our veins on quite possibly a daily basis.

Like those Wildebeest.

But in this heavily domesticated world we now live in.

With all our laws.

And boundaries.

And brick walls.

And even worse, fantastic pieces of technology and electronic gadgetry all designed to make us even lazier.

Or at least a lot less active.

We don't get those sudden dumps of adrenaline that we used to get back when we all lived in caves.

And so when this happens to us now, we're so not used to it that we don't know what to do.

And so we just simply freeze.

The massive amounts of adrenaline pumping through our veins overwhelms us so much that our legs feel like they've turned to jelly, we uncontrollably shake... and we do NOTHING with it.

Because we're not used to it.

I used to fight competitively many years ago and I remember stepping out onto the mats in my early days and not being able to get my arms and legs to do what I wanted them to do.

They just didn't work.

My legs felt like they had lead weights attached to them.

As did my arms.

And I'd gas out in seconds.

And let's not forget that I had trained for this.

I had spent many months preparing myself physically for the competition.

I was at my fittest.

My strongest.

My fastest.

I had spent hours and hours sparring in the luxurious confines of my Dojo.

Sparring in an environment I was comfortable in.

With people I knew.

And the only spectators being the few parents that were sitting around the edges of the room, generally reading a book, waiting for the class to finish so they could drive their son or daughter home again.

I was comfortable and safe and so there was no need for any adrenaline dump.

The only adrenaline surging through my veins was the natural adrenaline that comes with good old fashioned healthy exercise.

What I wasn't able to train or prepare myself for in these circumstances was the nerves.

The nerves brought about by being massively outside of my comfort zone.

Not really knowing anything about my opponent(s).

And having several hundred spectators watching my every move.

And it was all the fault of my body for dumping a whole load of adrenaline that caused those nerves the moment I heard my name called out and I stepped out onto the mat.

It also didn't help that the night before the competition I'd be nervous.

I'd be just as nervous on the drive to the event.

And I'd be even more nervous standing around and waiting for my category to be called out.

This kind of nervousness is the worst kind as your body picks up on your state of mind and in a feeble attempt at trying to help you, releases adrenaline slowly and constantly into the blood stream.

It's called 'slow release' adrenaline.

And you will have experienced it.

It's those butterflies in the stomach we get when we're anxious about something.

Maybe you have a big exam coming up in a week's time which you're worried about.

Or you have to do some public speaking.

Or even just going on a first date.

It's that kind of adrenaline we're all used to and it's being *used* to that that means we can still go ahead and do whatever it is we're anxious about doing.

It won't interfere with your performance in any way near as much as a huge dump of adrenaline will because there's only a small amount of adrenaline being released and it's being released slowly.

In fact most cases, it makes you a little more alert.

A little more aware.

Imagine standing under a waterfall and having the water trickle onto you.

You could deal with that no problem.

And then picture having the whole waterfall come crashing down onto you in one huge hit.

You'd be helpless.

The amount of adrenaline the body releases is directly proportionate to the level of stress it thinks you are going through.

Less stressful, prolonged situations equals slow release adrenaline.

Huge great stressful situations equals massive amounts of adrenaline.

And as quickly as possible.

But because we're not used to that amount of adrenaline being downloaded in one huge go, we can't deal with it as it's too much and so we freeze.

Some people refer to it as 'frozen with fear', but fear is not what has caused you to freeze, it's the adrenaline dump brought about by the fear.

Does that make sense?

Once I'd been fighting for a while I remember being able to do that thing that you often hear coaches tell their athletes....

'Control your nerves!'

And once you're used to dealing with nerves (adrenaline), then admittedly you are able to take back control of your body.

It's a bit like that other very popular saying....

'Face your Fear!'

All that really means is if you do something that scares you over and over again, if you don't die, eventually it won't scare you as much and so you are able to either enjoy or accept (depending on what it is) the experience a whole lot more because your subconscious (and even your conscious) mind will know you're not going to die and so will start to back off a bit.

I remember, back in my teens loving theme parks.

In fact the scarier the ride the more fun.

I was a true, white knuckle, thrill seeking, adrenaline junkie.

And then I found myself somehow becoming domesticated.

I settled down in a very secure relationship and started a home and a family.

And then, many years later, once the kids had grown up and were tall enough to not slip out of the seats, we headed back to the theme parks, and in particular, a rather tame ride that I forget the name of but you sat in it, it raised you up very high, and then span you round and round.

And I literally SH#T myself.

I held on to my harness with everything I had.

Even my toes somehow managed to grip the platform beneath me – through my shoes!

In fact I'm surprised they didn't have to crowbar me out of the seat once the ride had come to a complete stop.

My body sensed my anxiety and in a lame attempt at helping me, dumped a load of adrenaline into my blood stream which really didn't help in any way, shape or form and in fact, my fear of the ride coupled with this massive dump of adrenaline just made me think I was definitely going to die.

Now the kids are even older and we still go to theme parks and I always make a point of going on that same ride and can now hang there, upside down, waving my arms above (or rather, below) my head like a teenager without a care in the world and screaming with the best of them.

And how is this possible?

Because I'm used to it.

I've done it so many times now that I know I'm not going to die.

In fact there are bigger, scarier rides that I regular go on, which make *this* ride pale into insignificance and I now look back on my first time on this particular ride that terrified me thinking '*what was I afraid of?*'

So, how does my ability to go on a fairground ride help you deal with adrenaline dump?

Well the point of this whole chapter has been this.

The only way you can learn to deal with your fear of a street attack and be able to control the inevitable adrenaline dump that will occur for certain, is to put yourself in the exact same scenario that will induce that adrenaline dump, time and time again.

And the only way to do that, is to get yourself in a street attack over and over again until the fear subsides.

And who in their right mind is going to do that?

I read a great book once by a well known martial artist and expert on street survival and in it he explains how, in order to face his fear of being in a street attack, he become a doorman and security guard in some of the roughest parts of the country.

This was his way.

If you want to try to somehow learn how to control your body and mind during an adrenaline dump and don't want to work on a night club door in some of the roughest parts of the country then go off and do some mad, extreme, white knuckle type activities.

Standing at the edge of an open cage, your feet attached to a bungee cord, staring down at the ground hundreds of feet below you while some dude behind you in a vest top and blond highlights counts you down from 'THREE, TWO, ONE, GO!!!'

Now THAT'S adrenaline dump.

Or perching yourself over the edge of a perfectly good airplane doorway with nothing but a rucksack on your back with what is essentially a very large bed sheet inside that is (hopefully) going to stop you just plummeting those 15,000 feet to your death – and it wasn't even packed by you!

Now THAT'S adrenaline dump!

Your body *will* freeze and your mind *will* tell you not to move but you have to get past that if you're ever going to avoid being *'frozen with fear'*.

So to recap.

Adrenaline is natural.

And despite what you have just read, it *is* there to help you.

You can't really control it because it just happens.

You can only get used to it.

And then only to a certain extent.

But *that* might be all you actually need!

The BEST Form Of Defence

"What would you do if someone attacked you?!"

It's a question I've been asked all of my martial arts life by non martial art practicing individuals or early day students (students that are still quite new to the martial arts and still think there's some mystique and magic behind it all and hold anyone with a recognised Black Belt in the highest esteem) and to be honest, my answer has changed many times over the years.

And the reason it's changed many times over the years is because I've changed.

And I don't mean I've got better at martial arts so therefore I have invented some unstoppable move that can end a street confrontation instantly and so I'd definitely resort to my martial arts skills if ever I got attacked.

I mean… I've grown up.

Matured.

And, as much as I hate to admit I'm getting older, when you do get older, as a result of your life experience brought about through everything you have learnt, you do in turn get somewhat wiser.

We have four stages of learning as you know.

They are:

STAGE ONE
I don't know what I don't know (AKA Unconscious Incompetence)
        And it means just that. I'd like to learn to drive a car, but I haven't even begun to start the driving a car

process and therefore I haven't the foggiest how to do it or even what the hell all those levers do.

STAGE TWO
I now know that I don't know how to do this (AKA Conscious Incompetence).

Right, I've started learning to drive the car and realised it pretty damn hard to drive a car as there's just so much to take in. Incidentally, this is probably the toughest stage and the stage of learning where most people quit.

STAGE THREE
I know that I know how to do this (AKA Conscious Competence).

So I *can* actually drive this thing although there's still so much I have to think about *all* of the time. 'What do you mean mirrors, signal, manoeuvre?'

STAGE FOUR
I'm doing this thing now and can even retune the radio at the same time (AKA Unconscious Competence).

So I can drive a car and can do it naturally. I just jump in and drive without having to actually think about every individual, little thing.

Let me liken this now to the process that everyone studying a martial / fighting art goes through.

And I generalise….

Unconscious Incompetence.
I'm worried about being attacked therefore I'll start a martial art so that I can learn how to defend myself should I ever actually get attacked. Watching all those Jason Statham movies has made me realise that it really *is* possible to defeat ten men without even breaking a sweat, let alone getting hit and all of whom are top level fighters judging by the amazing jumping spinning kicks they're all

pulling off, oh and all of whom are also brandishing weapons!

Conscious Incompetence

So I've started studying with an instructor that promises he'll turn me into the next Jason Statham but OMG, this is harder than I thought it was going to be and why do you need to be able to do hundreds of burpees just to be able to punch someone in the face? But I've learnt a few good moves and so if anyone does attack me I'll just use one of those moves on them and that should be enough to end their fruitless attack as it works well on my completely compliant training partner.

Conscious Competence

Wow, I've been studying this Jason Statham street fighting art for quite time now and I now realise what little I knew in the previous stage (conscious incompetence). None of that stuff would have worked in a street attack (unless I got lucky or just happened to be attacked by a girl guide) as I really didn't know how to do it anywhere near as well as I can now and now that I know how to do it all properly and in turn know even more moves, and can almost touch my toes, I now know that if ever I do get attacked in the street I'd easily be able to defend myself, and maybe even against some multiple attackers as well, especially if one of them is carrying a knife. In fact a small part of me hopes that I *do* get attacked as I'll get a chance to try out my new found skills. Hope someone captures it all on their phone and uploads it to YouTube!

And I know you think I might be making this up now but I have seriously spent time with people on reality based training seminars who were hoping they'd actually get attacked on a night out so they could try out their new moves.

Unconscious Competence

What was I thinking? I've been studying this for long enough now to really understand that I knew nothing before. NOTHING! Plus I now realise that as a trained fighter we train and fight using rules and etiquette and as a result we're actually conditioned to react in a certain way unlike the street thug or mugger that DOESN'T abide by those same rules or etiquette and fights using sneaky underhand tactics and pure animal instincts and will think nothing of hitting you from behind with a metal bar when you're not expecting it and so the ONLY way I would actually ever try and 'fight back' if I found myself in a street confrontation now is if I absolutely couldn't avoid it altogether, walk (or better run) away, or give them the tangible object that they so desperately require. The ONLY way I would fight now is if my life, or the life of a loved one that just happens to be with me at the time, is in danger.

The most dangerous stage for anyone training in the martial arts is in the early stages of their training around the Conscious Incompetence stage) as it's in that stage that they think they know enough which of course in reality, they don't.

There's a reason motor insurance is a lot more expensive for new drivers.

The **Unconscious Competence** stage for anyone studying a 'fighting sport / art' takes many years to achieve and I'd even take the above example even further.

When I was really at the top of my game due to my age (being much younger than it is now), and testosterone, bravado, attitude and ego were all pumping through my head and veins I had a belief that I could easily defend myself should I ever find myself in a situation that required me *needing* to defend myself.

In fact in my youth and early martial art days I did indeed find myself nose to nose with some would be opponent and only a twitch away from a pub fight on several occasions, but luckily for me, my friends (or his) intervened before a single blow could be struck.

And I'd be way too quick to blast my car horn at anyone who dared do something that remotely caused me to have to break or slow down.

Luckily for me other than the odd two fingered salute, no one ever stopped and questioned me about it.

And I say luckily for me and not them, because I like to think of myself as a realist.

You see I have seen it for myself over many years.

People create a situation for themselves that they then can't verbally get out of (or choose not to) and the situation gets physical and they come worse off.

And this isn't just mouthy street yobs with no real fight training experience.

I've seen great sport fighters and / or martial artists get seriously injured because they completely underestimated their street wise opponent in *his* battle ground.

I've seen top level fighters, incredible physical specimens; crumble, because they just weren't really *mentally* prepared for a real life confrontation when it actually presented itself to them.

And I've even seen world class fighters at competition, fighters that you and I would look up to and hold in the highest esteem, get a bad call from a blind ref and in an instant the whole room has gone up and whereas seconds earlier these two amazing fighters were pulling off the most incredible moves with grace and ease, now the gloves were off and the haymakers were in full swing along with chairs, energy drinks and anything else these idiots and their club mates could get their hands on.

I noticed a bad review (one star) left by someone that had downloaded a self defence eBook with the comment that went something like 'load of crap, just join a martial art school'.

But the thing is a street attack is dirty.

It's vicious.

There are no rules to it.

As sport fighters and martial art practitioners we fight to rules.

And I know I'm going to upset a few of those traditional art practitioners now but as we don't all fight to the death using hand to hand combat on the battlefield anymore and instead those same traditional arts now compete in competition (some even in the Olympics -- you can't get a much bigger competition than that) therefore they are actually now 'Sport Martial Arts'.

With rules.

But a street thug doesn't.

A street thug doesn't have rules they need to abide by.

And they're not pre-condition to act (fight) in a certain way like a trained fighter / martial artist is.

Having been in and around the martial art / sport / fight world now for some thirty plus years I've have seen and experience quite a lot.

And my advice for those of you just starting out on your martial art / how to defend yourself from a street attack style journey, is to make yourself a cup of tea and head over to 'You Tube' type in '*Street Attack*', and watch what it throws up.

Gone are the days when your attacker would approach you from the front, engage you in polite conversation and then ask you if you'd be so kind as to hand over your wallet.

Street attacks can be fast, brutal and devastating and I don't care how many black belts you may have, if you can't see it coming there's nothing you can do about it.

I have so many stories about street attacks to tell that I could probably fill a whole other book with them all.

If someone is going to *really* attack you (or worse stick a knife in you), they're not going to tell you about it beforehand as there's a chance you may be able to do something about it.

I heard a harrowing story about a doorman that got stabbed to death because he'd refused someone entry to a nightclub.

The attacker placed his knife in a fast food paper bag and simply walked down the street, in full view of everyone with the knife concealed in the bag, walked up to the doorman, and then stabbed him to death through the bag.

The doorman didn't have a clue.

I have a friend that took some money out of a cash point in a town centre on a night out and woke up in hospital.

Due to his injury the surgeon assumed he must have been hit on the back of the head with a house brick.

He didn't even see his attacker.

'So… what would I do if someone attacked me at this stage in my life?'

You know what; it's a great question and one I honestly think has no *simple* answer.

There is no *'flow chart'* to follow.

No *'step by step'* guide you can refer to.

You could join a martial art school and assume the attitude of the guy that left the bad review (incidentally hiding behind a nickname) but if you're doing it because you want to learn how to defend yourself against a street attack then I'd give it at least ten years of regular training, several times a week, and with training partners that will push you and not hold back before you venture out doors.

Oh, and be sure to experience the nerves and adrenaline of competition as well, at least up until you are at a stage where you can control your nerves and adrenaline.

And if you opt instead to spend a lot of money on a self defence course then be sure you continue training everything you have learnt afterwards, otherwise you'll have forgotten it all within a few short months.

But I will tell you this in answer to the above question.

I know for sure that the one thing I would definitely do now if ever I found myself in a situation that *could* result in a street attack….

Anything and *everything* I possibly could to avoid ever having to answer that question for real. Which brings us nicely to….

Awareness

"I'm so confident now that I've been doing this self defence workshop that I've started taking a short cut through a field at night, which I'd have never done before."

I cringed when I heard this true story.

Luckily for the female involved I wasn't the only one.

I studied a reality based fighting system up to black belt level many years ago.

I won't name it because it's still being taught by the same people who just happen to be fantastic marketers but needless to say I really enjoyed some aspects of it, particularly the camaraderie and the bond I had with my fellow students, however large elements of what we were taught (in my opinion) had many flaws so I quit not long after getting my black belt... but that's not the point of this story.

The point of this story is that one of the female instructors decided to teach a six week workshop on women's self defence.

And she got a great deal of interest.

And after about week five, some of the women stayed behind to chat to the instructor (as the keen ones often do) and one of them happened to come out with the above statement... at about the same time that the chief instructor just happened to walk past.

And this guy was very much into this unique fighting art he had helped develop.

And also loved to prove a point.

And so he casually ambled over to join in the conversation.

"So you feel you could defend yourself if you got attacked now do you?"

"Definitely, these classes have been great and I'm a lot more confident now."

Now his female instructor, the one that was teaching the workshop, was a tough old cookie, so he grabbed hold of her, completely catching her by surprise, and threw her forcefully to the floor.

He then mounted her pinning her to the ground.

He then began slapping her around the face, hard shouting 'DO SOMETHING! COME ON, DEFEND YOURSELF, ESCAPE!'

She naturally panicked as she wasn't expecting this (who does) and all of a sudden it was turning quite serious (and nasty) and of course she desperately fought to get him off of her -- but without any luck!

This made him more determined to prove his point and so he began hitting (not slapping, *hitting*) her on the body, on the arms and on the legs all while still slapping her hard around the face.

She tried hitting him back, scratching him, pinching, biting, all the things she was teaching her class at the time but none of it was any good as he just kept grabbing her arms and shoving her face back into the floor every time she tried to do something and all the time while he still continuously hit her until eventually enough was enough and completely overwhelmed and helpless she let out one huge hysterical scream and erupted into floods of tears.

This snapped him out of his crazed, point proving attack just enough for her to scramble out from under him and sprint off into the changing rooms.

And he turned to his five wide eyed and open mouthed spectators from his kneeling position and calmly said.

"That's the reality of a street attack. You think you can deal with that?"

So needless to say the workshop ended one week earlier than originally planned.

And it *is* a true story, told to me by the very same female self defence instructor who incredibly said '*she learnt a lot from that experience.*'

I doubt very much if any of those women would have taken a short cut across a dark field at night *before* signing up to her course.

And none of what she taught them helped *her* in any way so in actual fact, this self defence workshop would have actually got someone seriously attacked, raped or murdered.

And in my opinion this is a huge problem.

Now don't get me wrong, I'm sure there are some great self defence courses out there run by experts that do know what they are talking about and from experience have tried and tested everything they teach, but how do you, the unsuspecting, non trained, humble member of the general public know this?

You don't.

I wouldn't know a good horse riding instructor from a bad one because I have no experience with horse riding.

I had the privilege of working with a highly respected martial arts instructor once.

I won't name him but he designed a knife defence programme that was so effective he was asked to teach it to the police.

He put it together after finding himself face to face with a knife wielding attacker and none of his previous knife defence skills worked and he ended up getting stabbed multiple times, mainly puncture wounds which are a whole lot worse than slashes.

The only reason he didn't die was because his girlfriend at the time was a nurse and was able to slow down his blood loss until the emergency services arrived.

Otherwise he *would* have died.

He then set about designing his own knife defence training programme based on his experience.

And, interestingly enough, his whole training programme was based around what you do *when* you get stabbed and not *if*.

And sure enough, during our training it became VERY apparent that if someone *intends* to stab you... you're definitely going to get stabbed.

His course was all about minimising the damage as best you can and living to tell and NOT doing some Hollywood style fancy kick and knocking the blade out of the attacker's hand... as is sometimes taught.

Try it for yourself.

Put on a white t-shirt, give a red marker pen to a friend and ask them to try to touch (stab) you with it and see how many red marks you end up with before you manage to restrain them.

So anyway, he recounted a story to me about visiting a very large martial arts show and watching a knife defence expert run a workshop about how to effectively deal with a crazed knife attack and was so appalled by what he witnessed he walked into the arena and stopped the seminar.

Obviously this didn't go down well as you can imagine however when he then offered to attack the knife defence expert with the knife in order to prove his point, the knife defence expert refused.

Again, probably not the best thing to do but having been on the receiving end of a knife attack and having almost died as a result and knowing that what this guy was teaching would get someone killed, he felt it was the right thing to do if not just to save one of those poor unsuspecting students from getting stabbed themselves.

And had this knife defence expert really believed in what he was teaching he would have surely be willing to demonstrate this (I would have thought) but he didn't.

Not only do people teach things on self defence courses that just wouldn't work but they teach ways of defending against attacks that just wouldn't happen.

That was the issue I had with a reality based fighting system I studied and consequently quit.

I hate quitting things, however we were learning five move combos on a compliant attacker (our training partner) while they stood there motionless having thrown their initial one punch attack, with their attacking arm still extended out for you all while they happily allowed you to attack them.

And this was at Black Belt level.

What very kind and considerate attacker throws one punch and then holds it out for you while you perform your five move combo on them.

We were taught how to catch a punch by the wrist and perform an arm break on the same arm.

Great in theory, but not in reality.

Get someone to throw a full speed punch at you, with retraction, and try to catch it by the wrist and see what happens.

And then if by some fluke you manage to do it, then instruct them to resist everything you then try to do to them all while giving them permission to hit you with the other spare hand, kick you if you're in kicking range, if not knee you, hard… or simply grab hold of you and start grappling.

It doesn't work!

But people still teach it.

I'd train privately, outside of the classes with some of the other students and when we tried to apply the principles we had been taught under pressure (pressure testing is quite important), none of it worked.

So let me ask *you* a question.

The answer to which will help you to reduce the chances of you ever having to defend yourself.

What's the difference between 'self defence and 'self protection'?

They both sound similar; however employing one over the other will give you a completely different end result....

So choose wisely!

Self defence is the bit that you have to do to defend yourself while someone is attacking you.

Self protection is the bit that you do *before* the attack in order to considerably reduce the chances of you actually getting attacked.

Let me say that again.

Self protection is about doing everything you can to considerably reduce the chances of you ever getting attacked.

Self defence is having done something (or everything) wrong, missed all the signs, ended up in the wrong place at the wrong time and now you're being attacked and have got to do something about it.

And most of it really is *common sense*.

I'll give you some examples.

Example Number 1
Don't take that short cut across a dimly lit field (or alleyway, or subway etc), at night even if it will shave a few minutes off your journey home. Opt for the longer, more populated and well illuminated route instead.

Example Number 2
Don't accept a lift off someone you don't know if you're on your own… and that includes taxi cabs unless they're from a reputable, licenced company that you have booked in advance and are travelling with friends.

Example Number 3
If you have to take money out of a cash point (particularly on a night out), do it with friends around you and certainly don't wander off on your own to do it.

Example Number 4
Don't wander into a pub you know nothing about. One of my students did this with some of his friends once and they all got beaten up.

Do you get the point?

Again I could write a whole book on *'what not to do'* but as long as you use your common sense, you'll greatly reduce the chances of ever getting attacked.

Apply a risk assessment to everything you do.

Yes, it might be a hassle but for just thirty seconds of thinking things through before you commit might just be enough to help you appreciate that yes, that quiet back street car park might be cheap, but when you come back to your car at night are you likely to get attacked?

And let's face it; most people do manage to get through the whole of their life never ever getting attacked.

It's normally always the other person that it happens to.

And you *may* just be one of those lucky ones.

Self defence and reality based instructors refer to using a colour code system.

WHITE equalling *'completely oblivious and almost walking around in a daze inviting someone to attack you'*.

And RED equalling *'walking around like you've sunk one too many Red Bulls and are just waiting for someone to attack you just like Inspector Clouseau waiting for Kato to jump out on him'*.

And all the varying shades of colours between white and red, all signifying different states of awareness.

Personally I don't think you need to know this and I've been on the courses *and* read the books and still can't remember all those different states of awareness, so to make things easier I'm always sure to be aware of where I am and who's around or approaching me.

And I don't mean, like the RED example above but I mean that if I'm out and about, day or night, home or abroad, regardless of where I may be, I'm always checking out who's around me and subconsciously grading them on how likely they are to attack me.

For example, I'm a little less worried about passing by a bunch of nerdy looking blokes in ill fitting suits all eating M&S sandwiches at lunchtime than I am if it's a group of stereotypical thuggish looking lads with their skin tight t-shirts, many of which have UFC or TAPOUT or BAD BOY or FULL CONTACT FIGHTER (you know the type) emblazoned on the front on a Saturday night after throwing out time.

In as much as I'm a little less worried about sitting down to eat in a nice, fancy restaurant than I am in a MacDonald's at 11pm on a Friday night.

Do you get what I'm saying?

It's like driving a car.

I make sure I'm always looking out of the windscreen, conscious of the fact that some idiot in the approaching lane may try to overtake and hit me head on, a child might run out in front of me, a pedestrian might step off the curb etc, etc.

What I don't do is drive down the road, at speed, texting on my phone, occasionally glancing up to check one of the ten road side signs I've just passed but really remaining completely oblivious as to what's happening around me and massively increasing my chances of writing my car off.

Like some people do.

Much like people *do* walk around in a daze all of the time.

Just be aware of where you are, your surroundings and who's around you.

And that doesn't mean that you can never enjoy going out again or you should treat everyone around you like potential murderers.

But just *be aware* and use your *common sense*.

I used to train with a reality based instructor that took this so far that he would walk out of an establishment if he couldn't sit in the corner of the room, his back to the walls, with more than one way out of the building and an exit close by.

He'd also carry a glass (had to be glass as it will do more damage) bottle of water and a good solid pen with him everywhere he went which he could use as a weapon if he ever got attacked.

Needless to say he didn't go out of his house much!

Avoidance

So if you increase your awareness you reduce your chances of getting attacked.

Now let's look at using AVOIDANCE to even further reduce your chances of getting attacked.

And the good news is, it's quite simple.

All you have to do is a few simple things like:

AVOID putting yourself in danger.

AVOID walking into that unknown pub.

AVOID walking past that rough looking bunch of yobs.

AVOID taking that short cut.

But most of all, AVOID ever *having* to defend yourself if you can, even if the time arises when you may well have to defend yourself.

And what I mean by that is that most of us have a relatively active sixth sense.

Most of us can sense when we're not really feeling comfortable about something.

In my younger, pub drinking days, I'd inevitably spot someone staring at me from across a crowded bar (and it was NEVER someone of the opposite sex -- damn you Hollywood!) and if I caught their hostile looking stare more than once I'd sneak out.

And sneak out not because I was scared worried or afraid but to simply reduce the chances of that person seeing me leave and following me into the car park.

Or if I was with a group of male friends, air my concern and then encourage them all to leave with me so we could go on somewhere else.

I was in Spain once on a reality based training weekend (we were invited out to train with our Spanish counterparts) and a group of us, all staying in the same hostel and all naturally English, decided to do the typically English thing and head out into the local town for some beer.

And naturally we ended up in a local, open air night club.

And we were the only non-Spanish in the whole of this night club.

And being typically English we were rather drunk.

And quite loud.

Now I was completely code WHITE, mainly because I was young, drunk, and stupid at the time and anyway the Spanish locals clearly weren't happy about us being there and one of our more switched on colleagues in the group suddenly noticed that we were surrounded, circled even, by pretty much all of the males in the club.

All of the women had vanished, even the female bar staff that had been serving us not that long ago (and we were all hanging around the bar area), so he made the judgement call to leave, along with the rest of us and as we headed for the exit through the parting waves of Spanish torsos, we got shoulder barged and shoved but it was the right call as the next day when recounting the story to our Spanish colleagues we were told just how lucky we were as it would definitely have kicked off as it does most nights without there being some fresh English meat to pound on and apparently all the locals carry blades so we would all been stabbed for sure.

Awareness coupled with common sense on that night certainly saved me from what would have been a serious attack.

But sometimes you might not want to walk away.

Well that's okay, but you then have to take your chances.

I, along with most of my students went out on our annual Christmas party last year.

I was propping up the bar, all Dell Trotter like, minding my own business and chatting to one of my female instructors when over my shoulder I heard someone announce… 'I 'ear your name's Bruce.'

Several in built, natural, threat level detection processes immediately started up -- and we're talking milliseconds here by the way.

To my right, slightly behind me was some guy, about 6' 3", crew cut, thuggish looking appearance.

In a millisecond my subconscious mind had categorized him and determined that he looked like the kind of guy that could lose his mind any minute and smash a glass in my face for no apparent reason… and he was unnecessarily engaging me in conversation, which I thought was both unnecessary and out of place.

And not polite small talk style conversation used to discover a common denominator, something we could both relate to and consequently build on so that we could then spend the night engaging each other in the most contemporary of conversation and eventually end up the best of friends -- for life.

No, instead he came out with some reaction inducing, stupid, nonsensical statement.

So, judging by the fact that he hadn't simply walked up and punched me in the back of the head my subconscious mind determined I had a few seconds at least.

Secondly, I couldn't see a glass or a bottle in his hand and he wasn't actually standing next to the bar or a table where his glass could have been within quick reaching distance so my subconscious mind was able to rule out the fact that he probably wasn't going to glass me.

He also wasn't holding anything in his hands so there was no chance of being instantly stabbed.

But he was talking to me and his tone of voice was somewhat rather provoking and his choice of words were a little strange, particularly as he didn't know me and as my name certainly isn't 'Bruce' then there must be some ulterior motive to his bothering me.

And the way he was standing was typical, street style open pose, hands down low by his side to give the appearance that he wasn't going to attack but in actual fact was primed and ready to send a big, John Wayne style, throw it from the hip, haymaker.

So my subconscious mind determined that he *was* a threat and passed all this information on to my conscious mind.

In a millisecond.

"I'm sorry" I replied as, still maintaining my casual, leaning on the bar and non threatening appearance, I turned (leaned) to face him.

I was still holding my bottle of beer in my right (dominant) hand with a relatively, *closed around the neck of the bottle style fist*, and was now leaning on my right elbow as I turned to face him thus meaning my right arm / fist was primed and I doubt very much he would have spotted it, and with my other hand I began to slowly scratch my head (which was actually setting up my lead hand into some kind of defensive guard position) but the curious expression on my face would have led him to believe I was a bit confused (like Stan Laurel) which is exactly what I wanted him to think as me acting non threateningly, casual and somewhat confused would have meant he didn't see me as a threat -- which I wanted.

"Yeah, apparently your name is Bruce, like Bruce Lee, and you fancy yourself as a bit of a fighter and you could 'ave me!"

Through my peripheral vision I could see that EVERYONE in my immediate vicinity was a student of mine.

Plus, one of the two heavy set doormen was the father of one of my junior students.

So I knew in the back of my mind that if this all did kick off it would be stopped in seconds, so as much as that made me feel somewhat more secure, seconds is really all that is required for one of us to get really, seriously hurt.

So I remained vigilant.

I smiled, "I think you've got me mistaken with someone else my friend."

I figured the smile coupled with '*my friend*' would be quite a relaxed and even welcoming approach and his subconscious mind may well go on to think that we may just be friends -- at least for a little bit anyway.

"Apparently you're a kickboxer and think you're really 'ard and you could kill me with your bare hands!" he smirked.

I gestured to myself "Look at me, do I look like I'm really hard?"

Luckily I don't and I figured if I draw his attention to that fact he might agree with me and not see me as his next challenge.

He didn't take me up on my kind invitation to 'check me out' and instead continued to maintain his threateningly, ice cold stare.

"Yeah, well it's the ones that don't look much that you have to watch out for!"

BRILLIANT!

Just then one of my students caught my eye from over his shoulder and shouted over 'Wanna a drink?'

I heard his kind offer, clearly, but pretended not too and instead in a rather loud voice shouted back 'Sorry mate, what was that?'

Tough Guys clocks this, and also clocks that my student was stood in a rather large group and my student heads over to join me so I now stand up straight, swap my bottle into my other hand and greet him with a friendly cup of the arm with my right hand, but what I'm actually doing is positioning him in between myself and Tough Guy thus creating a barrier between us and by keeping my student's head in between mine and his, I break line of sight with him.

I then engage my student in conversation completely blanking out Tough Guy in order to subconsciously signal to Tough Guy that our conversation is now over, all while keeping Tough Guy in my peripheral vision… just in case.

Luckily for me Tough Guy hangs about for a few more seconds and then realising that I'm not going to bite walks away while my female comrade, who knew the doorman really well, went and had a quick word and got him thrown out.

And that was that.

And so the point of this story was that I could have approached the situation much differently.

I could have squared up to him.

Challenged his opinion of me.

But where would that path have led us both?

Most probably not where it did end up.

And even if we did get physical.

If I somehow managed to put a stop to any physical attack he threw my way.

I could never really visit that pub again without always worrying if I was going to bump into him again.

I'd rather do whatever I could do to avoid the possibility of it all kicking off and then I could enjoy the rest of the night instead of running the risk of having to spend the night in a jail cell, a hospital bed or waiting for that inevitable knock on the front door.

So avoidance doesn't just mean avoiding all the possible places that you could find yourself in which could result in you getting attacked.

A huge part of avoidance means that if you *do* ever find yourself in a situation, face to face with someone that wants to hurt you, do everything and anything you can to avoid the situation from becoming physical… if you can.

If someone is prepared to stab you unless you give them your wallet, watch, phone… in my opinion, give it to them.

The thing is though you can never account for any and every possible situation.

I've heard stories about someone spilling someone's drink, apologising, offering to buy them another and getting put in hospital.

And I've also heard stories about someone spilling someone's drink, apologising, buying them another and everyone's happy.

I've always followed this principle system below.

It works for me but please be aware that what works for one, may not necessarily work for another.

Everyone is different so maybe consider creating a principle system that works for you.

Principle one
Be aware at all times.

Principle two
Avoid getting yourself into a sticky situation in the first place.

Principle three
Go with your gut instinct.

Principle four
Adopt the Road House philosophy -- Always be nice.

I read a story in the paper once about a guy that was beaten to death (to DEATH) by a motorist because he didn't say thank you when the motorist stopped to let him cross at a zebra crossing.

Smile.

Apologise.

Do whatever you can to keep the situation calm.

This isn't about ego, it's about not getting hurt or killed.

Some people suffer from a guilt complex which prevents them from doing this because they'd then feel like a failure because they didn't stand up for themselves.

It's a dangerous gamble but as I say, being nice is what works for me and I've managed to prevent a lot of potentially dangerous situations from turning bad by acting humble and not reacting when someone questions my manhood.

Principle five
Get outta there. If you feel threatened, don't hang around.

If you feel it is going to turn physical, you are going to get stabbed then get the hell out of there.

Run if you have to.

Make as much noise as possible and head for somewhere populated.

It's also much harder for someone to hit you if you're moving away from them at a rapid rate.

Principle six (if you *can't* or choose not to *'get outta'* there)
Do everything you can to *talk* your way out of the situation… but keep principle eight in the forefront of your mind.

I had a friend with the gift of the gab that could talk his way out of anything.

He once managed to talk his way out of throwing a pint of beer over a bunch of thuggish looking guys in a nightclub (he was aiming for me and I moved).

Anyone else would have got the kicking of their life, but not him.

And he didn't even need to buy any of them a drink.

You're *less* likely to get hit while you keep someone engaged in polite, courteous conversation.

Principle seven
Give them whatever tangible objects their asking for.

I can't really think of any reason why your late mother's necklace or your £5,000 Rolex is worth more than your life.

Again, that's just me.

Principle eight
If you don't think you're going to be able to talk your way out of it (and you may well come to that decision without ever uttering a word).

If they want YOU and *not* your money or jewellery.

You can't run away.

And they're NOT carrying a weapon.

And you're not surrounded.

Use a full on, no holding back, all you can give, pre-emptive strike (more on that soon) with the possibility of several more if you have to.

Principle eight
They pull out a weapon.

Refer back to the earlier principles and consider using these to begin with.

If you can't for whatever reason and you believe your attacker is going to use the weapon then you need to find an equaliser.

And I'm not referring to Edward Woodward now… an equaliser in this situation is something you can use that equalises the odds.

For example, they pick up a bottle, you pick up a bottle -- that kind of thing.

They have a knuckle duster -- you place your car key between your knuckles.

They have a knife -- you take off your belt and swing the buckle end around.

Even holding your coat by the sleeve and swinging that around gives you some kind of equaliser and is better than nothing.

Or a bag.

Throwing either at them will give you a second to run away.

Now, here's the thing.

This is all well and good if it's a stereotypical type of confrontation.

However, everything changes if your confronted by a gang because, as much as I love him, even Jason Statham would struggle to take out two guys (let alone ten) that wanted to do him some harm in the real world.

People just don't patiently wait to attack you one at a time in the real world.

Have a look on You Tube if you don't believe me.

Being faced with a gun completely changes everything.

Try Googling *'Defence against a gun'* and see how *few* text based entries there are.

There are a few videos of a people showing you how to defend yourself when faced with a gun at close range, but would you really risk it if all they wanted was your wallet?

And what do you do when facing a gun pointed at you from a distance?

No one shows that on You Tube.

I remember watching a TV programme once and the highlight of this show was that a highly skilled martial arts master was going to disarm someone brandishing a samurai sword, with his bare hands.

Now this I had to see.

The antagonist and the protagonist face off.

The antagonist raises the samurai sword high above his head and holding it in both hands brings it downwards, targeting the very top of the protagonists head... VERY slowly.

And the protagonist simply claps his hands together, trapping the blade in between the palms of his hands and thus, disarming the attack.

It was truly the most ridiculous thing I had ever seen.

Let *me* swing that sword at him and then see if he can catch it by simply clapping his hands together.

The other thing to consider is that if your attacker is suffering from mental health issues, is high on mind altering drugs or just even high on alcohol, *everything* changes.

I watched a '*CCTV footage show*' recently where six police officers tried to restrain someone on mind altering drugs and he threw them all around like rag dolls.

I know of a highly respected, tough as nails, reality based instructor that got attacked completely out of the blue by someone on mind altering drugs and the fight lasted several minutes (which may not seem a long time but try fighting at 100% for several minutes when someone with several times your strength that feels no pain and just won't stop, is *literally* trying to kill you and tell me that's not tough) and despite the instructor hitting his attacker so hard and so many times that he managed to cave in both of his attackers eye sockets so his attacker couldn't even see him, it didn't stop him.

That's not the kind of confrontation anyone wants.

Ever!

So before you even need to consider throwing your first punch, adding AVOIDANCE in with AWARENESS may prevent things getting physical and may just help you live another day!

The Pre-Emptive Strike

We're taught that if someone hits you, hit them back.

Not always a great philosophy but it's what we're taught.

And not always a great philosophy not because this philosophy insinuates that you have to wait to be hit before you can defend yourself, but because hitting someone back just *because* they hit you *could* land you in a whole heap of trouble.

More on this later.

What we're not taught however is to hit someone first.

Hit them *before* they've hit you.

Before they even raise a fist.

Even a lot of traditional fighting arts still base their training on the '*block and counter*' approach.

Block an attack, and then hit back.

So a pre-emptive strike does exactly that thing that our parents, our schooling, our environment and society tell us NOT to do.

Hit first!

And that's great, but hitting someone isn't an easy thing to do for the majority of us.

Even some trained martial artists have a problem with punching someone in the face, with their bare knuckles, outside of the training environment.

And even if we could punch someone in the face without any remorse, we've had every conceivable law passed to prevent us from actually punching someone in the face.

We know that if we are to punch someone in the face, there's a very good chance there would be consequences.

I know of many people that have hit someone in self defence only to end up themselves with a criminal record.

So here's the thing....

In the eyes of the law, if you believe someone is going to do you harm, you are allowed to defend yourself by striking first.

See http://www.cps.gov.uk/legal/s_to_u/self_defence/#Pre-emptive for more information from the official Crown Prosecution Service website.

That said, this isn't as simple as being black and white and instead is a *very* grey area as you'll see if you've looked at the site.

So my advice, before you go round punching anyone that looks at you a little weird, is to seek out the professional advice of someone that knows the law very well.

The crown prosecution service website has a whole section dedicated to self defence -- but it's still a *huge* grey area.

And I would hate to give you advice that gets you into trouble, so here's *my* humble opinion on the whole '*hitting someone first*' situation.

Having spoken to many police officers (I have a lot that train with me) and solicitors (I have a few that train with me) about the whole self defence and pre-emptive strike situation, as well as reading up on several professional websites, books and martial art magazines that feature columns on this very subject....

If I believed someone was going to hurt me, physically, and there was no way I was going to be able to walk or talk my way out of the situation or give them my wallet, I would strike first and hope that that was enough to either provide me with an opportunity to escape, or to end the confrontation and consequently the danger.

If one pre-emptive strike wasn't enough and I felt that my attacker would continue their attack on me, I'd send a second one.

If that wasn't enough, I'd send a third.

I'd basically keep sending attacks until the threat of danger had been neutralised, or I was able to make good my escape.

And here's something to consider....

THE ESCAPE.

I know in this day and age we're all good Samaritans and consequently you might want to stick around and wait for the police to arrive or even see how your attacker is doing now that you've laid them out, but it might not be your best move.

I know of several situations where a victim has hung around after they managed to end their attack only to have the attacker recover and attack them again.

I know of someone who actually bent down to try to issue first aid to their attacker and ended up being dragged down onto the floor with them and consequently over powered and seriously hurt.

So once you've given yourself the opportunity to escape… ESCAPE!

If the police want to speak to you about what happened they'll find you.

Or if you feel you need to do the right thing then report it.

But I'd advise that you leave the danger scene ASAP and then deal with everything else once you are completely safe.

So how much force do you use?

It's a good question and again I refer you back to that *grey* area, although you might argue that this *could* actually be a black and white answer.

You see, the Crown Prosecution Website indicates that '*A person may use such force as is reasonable in the circumstances…*'

Reasonable force.

But what's reasonable?

What's considered reasonable in my eyes may not be reasonable in the eyes of the twelve jurors residing on my court case.

What's considered reasonable in *your* eyes might not be considered reasonable in the eyes of all your witnesses.

So here's *my* opinion on it once again.

If I believed I was about to be attacked and I couldn't walk away or talk my way out of the situation I would strike first, as fast as I could (to increase the chances that my self defence related, pre-emptive strike was effective) and as hard as I deemed necessary to end my attack with just one strike.

If that ended the confrontation then I would do no more.

What I then *wouldn't* do, under any circumstances, is hit my attacker again.

And again.

And again.

Reasonable force, when referring to a self defence situation, refers to doing the *minimum* amount of everything that is required to bring a confrontation and potential (or actual) attack to an end.

The minimum amount of power combined with the minimum amount of strikes.

And here's where the grey area kicks in.

The minimum amount of force required to stop a twenty stone, muscle bound thug from trying to kill you is probably going to be somewhat different compared with the minimum amount of force required to stop an eight stone geek.

The geek may only need one punch.

The twenty stone thug may need a little more.

If a women was attacked by a twenty stone, drug fuelled, rapist and somehow managed to hit him around the side of the head with a rock, which consequently killed him, in the eyes of the law, that might be considered *reasonable*.

The thing to consider in all of this is what YOU consider to be reasonable as it's YOU on the receiving end of an attack and as long as you can say that you '*honestly believed*' your life was in danger and what you did was the '*minimum you felt you needed to do*' then that is YOUR opinion therefore very difficult to disprove as it's what YOU believed at that exact moment in those exact circumstances.

Does that make sense?

Reasonable cannot be quantified as it's all circumstantial but the most important thing to understand here is not *what you do* but rather *what you say* that will determine whether you are convicted of GBH or get let off.

A police friend of mine told me a story of how someone high on drink and drugs smashed a glass into someone's face in a pub on a night out.

The attacker then ran out of the pub, followed closely by his victim who managed to catch hold of him and beat him senseless.

When it went to court the *victim* got sent down because the judged considered that the attacker had ended his attack at the point where he ran off and that's where it should have all finished.

The fact that the victim then chased him down the street, catching hold of him and carrying out his 'revenge' meant that the victim then became the attacker and the attacker became the victim.

We can all sympathise with the glassing victim in this case and perhaps we might have considered doing the exact same thing if it were us in that same situation, however this is a great example of how the law works and how you have to be very careful in situations like this.

If it's of any help whatsoever, we do have a saying in the self defence world.

'Better to be judged by twelve than carried by six'

If your life is in danger, there's a chance you could get seriously physically and / or mentally scarred or even killed by your attacker, don't give it a second thought.

Do everything and anything you can to defend your own life and then simply deal with any consequences that may arise as a result of you defending your life, afterwards.

Better to have the luxury of a trial in front of a jury of twelve people than be carried to your grave in a coffin by six.

Areas Of Attack

There are several points on your attacker's body that you can aim for which will greatly increase your chances of ending their attack a lot quicker.

The thing is though....

One, you really only get one shot at this.

Two, your targeting needs to be really good to hit that spot.

Three, you run the risk of knowing too much, suffering from information overload and as a result, over think things, not decide quickly enough about where on your attacker you're going to hit, and your attacker beats you to it.

I remember many years ago buying a poster entitled 'Karate Striking Points' and it showed a drawing of a guy in his pants standing in a Karate style pose with all the areas on the body you could attack highlighted and the striking tools you can attack with detailed at the bottom, and it looked great.

Except there was too much information on it.

You see we have a zillion techniques available to us in the martial arts.

More if you cross train.

And the thing is, most great fighters only use a few.

One of my all time heroes, back when I was first learning, was a guy called Bill 'Superfoot' Wallace (Google him) and I've had the privilege of attending several of his seminars over the years and on one seminar I asked him about his favourite technique and he told me that during all twenty three of his kickboxing victories he only used five techniques.

A left jab.

A lead hook.

A lead side kick.

A lead round kick.

And a lead hook kick.

And he could hit you with all of them anytime he wanted.

In his book, 'Watch My Back', Geoff Thompson explains that he ended the vast majority of his confrontations with a perfectly lined up punch to his opponents jaw.

Just one technique is all he used and if you Google him you'll see he's studied several different styles of fighting art to very high levels so knows loads of techniques.

So here's the thing.

I could go the way of that Karate poster and list everything.

Or make this book even bigger; provide you with more information and charge more for it.

But I don't think I need to.

Because I don't think YOU need to know too much information otherwise I believe you run the risk of suffering from information overload.

So I'll give you just a few key areas to focus on instead.

Let's start from the top and work our way down.

At the very top we have the **EYES**.

Give everything above the eyes a miss because you'll either run the risk of breaking your hand or you need to be one hundred percent accurate, and I'm going to say that in the heat of a very heated moment you probably won't be.

The eyes are an incredibly delicate and sensitive part of the body and as such, try touching someone on the head and see what they do and then do the same thing with their eyes and see how differently they react.

I accidentally shoved my right thumb into my training partner's left eye while on a reality based training weekend a while back.

We were actually practicing thumb jabs to the eye and in a moment of distraction I moved in to simulate my attack at the exact same time as he moved in and my thumb went straight into his eye socket.

And it was horrific.

It was like shoving my thumb into jelly.

He screamed like nothing I've ever heard before and dropped to his knees in so much pain that he couldn't open *either* of his eyes.

And I hadn't even touched his right one.

Anyway, I eventually managed to help him over to the side of the training room where he sat, with his palm pressed into his left eye in an attempt to ease the pain, still unable to open his eye for several hours, while the training continued.

At the end of the session he was still in so much pain and still unable to open his eye that I took him to A&E where they sent him straight to an eye specialist.

He returned an hour or so later with a huge bandage on his injured eye and a course of pills and drops that he had to take for several days.

He was unable to see out of his eye for the rest of the weekend (even without the bandage) and in fact, unable to do anything.

When I bumped into him several months later he had made a full recovery and there was no damage to his eye whatsoever -- which I was very grateful about.

Needless to say we haven't trained together since.

And as horrific as it was to cause him so much suffering, especially as I really liked him, I did think to myself at the time '*that worked well!*'

And so for your reference and peace of mind, it is a medical fact that you can shove a digit into someone's eye socket so deep that you push their eye ball all the way back until it hits the very rear of their eye socket with a very small risk of causing any permanent damage.

....

I'm going to suggest the **NOSE** next as it follows down but *only* if you find yourself grabbed from behind in a bear hug style grab and you can head butt your opponent on it using the back of your head.

It might be enough to cause them to momentarily relax their grip on you giving you a vital opportunity for escape.

Otherwise as this won't knock anyone out and some people can just shake off a solid strike on the nose I'd avoid hitting this area when there are other areas I believe to be *much* more effective.

....

The **JAW** is my second favourite place to hit as a good solid shot anywhere along the jaw line has the possibility of knocking your attacker out cold.

There are however several dangers here to take into consideration.

One, even though it's a relatively large area you still need a degree of accuracy to hit the jaw line, especially in the heat of the moment.

Two, as you are striking a solid bone with your bare hands there's a risk of injury to your hand.

If you break your hand at this point and the shot doesn't knock out your attacker, you've lost your best weapon.

*On that note, my latest ebook '**Knock Someone Out With ONE Punch'** is now available on Amazon. Have a quick look if you'd like to know how to actually knock someone out with one punch.*

Three, there's a huge risk that if you are lucky and knock your attacker out, they fall and hit their head on the floor or a curb.

If someone hits their head on the floor, or a curb, there's a very high risk of serious injury or death.

I know of several people that this has happened to and it's never a pleasant experience.

And **Four**, you're going to have to line the shot up in order for it to work.

….

The **THROAT** is an area you wouldn't necessarily think of however in the Martial Arts (Military / Battlefield Arts), where the whole purpose on a battlefield is to finish a fight as quickly as possible, the throat is considered a major striking area.

An old acquaintance of mine, who used to enjoy a good street fight, used to only target the throat of his opponent and he informed me that one solid blow always ended his fights instantly.

….

Let's move down the body now and assume it's the height of summer.

If you attacker is wearing a thick coat avoid targeting the body.

I've seen a firearms officer fire his taser into the body of someone wearing a thick winter coat and it did nothing, so a punch to the mid section on this occasion would be fruitless.

If, however, your attacker is wearing a t-shirt and the face is unavailable for whatever reason, then you could consider these two mid line striking areas.

The **SOLAR PLEXUS**, is that bit of the body where the ribs join -- the top of the wishbone if you like.

There's very little protection so a good solid blow in this area can sometimes down an opponent.

I've been hit there in sparring and it does drop you instantly.

I've also hit many people there with incredible (and satisfying) results.

....

The **LIVER** is also an area on the body to consider attacking.

It is situated on the right side of the body so be sure to mirror this when facing someone.

A good solid shot in the liver has the potential to end a fight instantly.

Interestingly, Bill Wallace informed me that the vast majority of his knockouts were as a result of him hitting someone in the body, particularly the liver, and not the head.

....

Let's go a bit lower still and focus on the **GROIN**.

I've lost count as to the number of people, when learning that I train, inform me that it's all crap and a good solid kick in the groin is all you need to end a fight.

We're led to believe that this target area is one hundred percent effective, but it might not always be the case.

Behind the groin sits solid bone so you need to be careful how you attack this area to reduce the risk of injury to yourself (more on that in the next chapter).

Plus, there's an inherent risk that clothing may create additional padding.

Or as you commit to your attack, your attackers leg, knee or other limb gets in the way thereby obstructing your attack.

....

The **SHIN** is an easy target to strike on an upright opponent because it's low to the ground and if you kick they may not even see it coming.

It's made up of a serrated bone with multiple nerve endings.

A good solid blow to the shin can cause immense pain and temporarily disable an attacker thus preventing them from chasing you.

....

And last of all I'm going to include the **FOOT** because if you find yourself grabbed from behind, a good solid stamp on someone's foot could be enough to release their grip on you.

Just be sure they're not wearing steel toe capped boots though.

So there you have it.

There *are* lots of other striking areas you could target but here's my take on it.

Don't be a collector of techniques, or in this case… targets.

Just like those great fighters with their minimal number of attacking techniques, I believe it's far better to limit your options to just a few so that if ever you do need to defend yourself, you haven't got to go through a huge checklist in your mind.

But which of those is the best area to hit?

I think it better for you to aim for the easiest target with the least resistance.

If I tell you to only target the jaw, as a good solid blow can cause a knockout and ideally that's what you want, and then you find yourself faced with a 6' 6" giant, and you're just 5' 8", you won't even be able to reach their jaw, let along hit it with enough power to generate a knock out.

So aim for the easiest target for YOU.

If they're the same height as you but wearing a motorbike helmet you obviously won't target the head.

If you're planning on targeting the eyes but your attacker has shades or glasses on, you may need to re-think your strategy.

If your attacker has a thick winter coat on, forget attacking the body.

On the same hand, if you're not confident about punching someone in the jaw, then you may need to start re-thinking your strategy and perhaps practice kicking shin height instead.
Now let's take a look at what you use to actually hit with….

Your Natural Weapons

Let's strip away all those thousands of martial arts moves and stick to the very basics.

Also consider that all of the books, videos, seminars on self defence are produced by self defence *experts*, with their wealth of expertise and experience.

Plus, they've spent years learning how to fight, honing their skills, conditioning their bodies and working on their technique.

You (probably) haven't.

One of my all time favourite kicks is a spinning back kick.

According to '*The Science of Martial Arts*' documentary I watched it is the most powerful of all kicks.

In the hands of a real expert I believe it *could* be lethal.

If ever I'm sparring with someone that is getting a bit too big for their boots and should know better and they have chosen to ignored all my warnings (to calm down) I'll send a spinning back kick into their mid section and nine out of ten times it stops the fight.

INSTANTLY!

If they are lucky enough to block it, it generally still stops the fight as they then can't lift their arm back up again, let alone actually use it to hit me with.

The way you perform a spinning back kick is as follows:

Face your target / opponent / training partner / attacker in a side facing fighting stance.

You *can* use it from a front on fighting stance but you need to do more work, plus you also run the risk of the kick going wrong.

Twist your feet so that you literally turn your back on your target / opponent / training partner / attacker.

If done correctly you will now find that your kicking leg is in front of you -- almost like you are doing a front facing fighting stance in the opposite lead.

Check over your shoulder -- the shoulder you twisted with.

Chamber your kicking leg as if you are about to do a front kick (in front of you).

Then bring your kicking leg in a perfectly straight line, directly under your body, thrusting it through with your hip for additional power and leaning slightly with it for extra energy.

Be sure to strike with the heel or the foot sword and keep the foot in a side on position when it connects with the target.

Also be sure to keep your back towards the target throughout the whole final stage of this kick and when you land, jump straight back into your fighting stance to minimise the length of time you have your back to your target / opponent / training partner / attacker.

Did you get all of that?

I'll be very surprised if not only did that make no sense whatsoever, but you could actually pull it off to any degree.

Let alone use it to stop someone.

Yet people advise you use it as an effective self defence move.

I have advanced level students that still can't pull it off properly due to the complexity of it.

So what chance does someone have a pulling it off that has absolutely no kicking experience?!

I'm more of a stand up fighter and have been taught some great throws on many of these seminars but I couldn't tell you how to do them now.

The reason for this is because I simply don't practice them.

Plus, they were quite complex moves.

And by the way, I would strongly advise against you trying a spinning back kick on an attacker unless you can pull one off effortlessly, with incredible speed and timing, in every possible situation.

I've been doing spinning back kicks for the past thirty years.

I can hit you with it from close range (chest to chest).

From a distance.

With my eyes closed.

And I probably wouldn't attempt a spinning back kick in the street.

And here's another thing to consider.

You'll always do what you can do.

People say a head kick is ineffective in the street, yet I've seen many people get knocked out with a kick to the head -- in the street.

People say not to get into a grapple in the street, but if you practice Judo, this is exactly what you'll do because you need to grab hold of your opponent in order to throw or restrain them.

People say don't let a fight go to the ground but I've watched a Brazilian Jiu Jitsui fighter go straight to the ground *and* win the fight.

So you'll do what you can do.

If you're *not* a trained fighter I would certainly recommend you stick to the target areas detailed in the previous chapter and focus on just a couple of the weapons included in this chapter.

To take on too much information and attempt something outside of your natural range and capability would be seriously detrimental to your health and safety.

So let's look at what I consider to be the best weapons to use to potentially end a fight or attack in one move.

….

The Eye
An incredibly effective weapon to use to target the **EYE** is your finger or thumb.

However, set up and targeting is key with this and as easy as you may think it is to jab a finger into an eye socket, think again.

Stick a ping pong onto the end of a piece of string and pin or stick it to the ceiling so that it dangles down about head height.

Then practice jabbing it, in the same way as you would if you were doing it for real, with your finger or thumb.

If you can manage to hit the exact centre of it every single time then brilliant, you are clearly a natural.

But I suspect that may not be the case and instead it's spinning off in all directions.

Now try thrusting all of your digits at the ping pong ball all together and see what happens.

Much more effective.

Just be aware that three things may well happen if you decide to use this technique.

One, you land a perfectly placed digit into the eye socket of your opponent and end the fight.

You can then choose to make good your escape or send a second technique if you believe it is needed.

Two, you're unsuccessful in your attack but you instigate a reaction in your opponent (a flinch or turn of the head for example) which then leads the way for you to send a second strike which could then end the attack.

Three, you miss or it doesn't have the desired effect and now you have a problem.

My advice therefore, would be this.

Use the fingers of your lead hand to target your attacker's eyes (more on this in the next chapter).

The reason for this is that you don't need to strike the eyes with everything you've got.

You could easily stick the little finger of your weakest hand in a bowl of jelly and have it go right to the bottom.

Plus, speed is the key with this so if you've *'built your wall'* correctly (next chapter), then your weakest hand is naturally going to be nearest to your attacker's eyes.

If you miss, or something goes wrong you are potentially set up to send the all powerful punch using your (now set up) power hand, straight to their jaw (*don't forget to check out my other book, but only if you want to of course* ☺)

The key thing with a miss or an unexpected result is to keep going.

Ideally hit with everything you've got.

Become the Loony Tunes Tasmanian Devil.

You are far more likely to then land something that does the job, or as evidence shows, you're more likely to survive an attack if you fight back than if you don't.

Let's just touch on *Animal Instincts* for a brief moment here.

We all have the survival gene.

It's in us naturally.

So if someone seriously harmed your child.

Or someone else you care for just as much.

And you got hold of them….

You'd kill them.

Even if you don't know how to fight or defend yourself you'd use what we call *'Animal Instincts'* to get the job done.

Animals aren't taught how to fight, or defend themselves, it's in them naturally.

What we tend to do as human beings, living in this domesticated world we all now live in, is undo our natural inbuilt instincts.

We can all swim naturally as babies but the longer we leave it before throwing ourselves in water, the greater our fear of drowning and so instead of just doing what is naturally in us and swim, we panic… and drown.

We *can* all fight.

It's in us naturally.

But because we don't need to anymore we forget how.

And then what *stops* us from defending ourselves in most cases when we need to is the *fear* of being hurt or being killed.

The *fear* is far worse than the *actual*.

A lot of my students are afraid to spar because deep down they're really afraid of the pain of being punched in the face.

But having taught people to fight / spar for over twenty years, when it happens most of them discover that it's not actually as bad as they thought it was going to be.

Most people can take a bare knuckle full contact punch to the face.

It's only when it hits them square on the jaw do they get knocked out.

And this isn't due to the pain.

It's due to the affect this has on the brain as it bounces around inside the skull.

It's just natural biology (check out my new book if you want to know *why* we get knocked out -- am I plugging that a bit too much now???).

And it doesn't have to be a particularly hard punch either.

Just a well placed punch.

You see generally the body is very resilient.

Especially when adrenaline is pumping round it.

I've seen CCTV footage of people getting shot, several times, and still managing to run away.

Admittedly they've needed medical assistance afterwards (the body's not *that* resilient) but they've still managed to run to safety first.

Only recently I watched CCTV footage of a thief in a jewellery store try to rob the place.

The store owner pulled out a gun, activated the electronic locking system on the door and then unloaded the whole magazine into the thief as he scrambled around the floor of the shop on his hands and knees desperately trying to get away.

Then once the magazine was empty the store owner proceeded to pistol whip the thief with the gun as he begged for his life.

The police arrived within minutes and the thief was arrested but he survived the attack -- with several bullets in him.

Don't get me wrong, there are a lot of people that die from gunshot wounds but the main point I'm trying to make here, and I really need you to understand this, is that **failure to act through '*a fear of being hurt*' could be your biggest mistake** and either get you (seriously) hurt, or killed.

The body is incredibly resilient so if there's the slightest chance that you're going to get hurt or killed anyway, why hold back?

....

The Jaw
Target the **JAW** with a punch from your strongest hand.

Your strongest hand is normally the one you write with.

I know I said you don't need to hit the jaw all that hard to get a knockout but your strongest hand is still going to be the best one to use and will feel more natural to you.

For example, you can still write with your weaker hand but it just won't feel right or perform as well, so you'll generally always use the best hand for the job.

Ideally the punch needs to travel from its starting position to your attacker's jaw as quickly as possible and with as much power as you *can* muster up, so if you've built your wall properly, you should be in the best position to strike from.

The punch needs to connect anywhere on the jaw line to have an effect.

If you aim for the middle of the jaw, then you have a greater chance of hitting than if you aimed for the chin and then missed.

Now here's the thing….

You might not know how to throw a punch.

That doesn't matter (*you could always check out my new book. Sorry! That was the last time, I promise!*)

I've witnessed many fights; either for real or on CCTV and I can tell you for certain that that most people don't either.

Punches thrown in panic and under stress and pressure are more a case of a frenzied flailing of arms.

All you need to be able to do is make a fist.

To do that, extend your arm, holding your palm facing down towards the ground.

Close your fingers tightly into your palm ensuring your thumb is on the outside and tucked under the bottom of your fingers.

There's much debate in the martial arts world as to which part of the fist you strike with.

Do you use the first two knuckles (the index or the middle) or the last three (middle, ring and little).

Who cares -- just hit them!

Word of warning though….

If you hit with the little finger knuckle on its own you'll likely break your hand.

You may still get the knockout but you'll still likely break your hand.

If it happens then deal with it afterwards.

Do everything you can to try NOT to hit with your little finger knuckle but don't spend so much time worrying about it to then do nothing.

The Filipino stick fighters are prepared to have their arm broken by their opponents stick in order to get the head (kill) shot, so take a leaf out of their book.

If you do break your hand but get the knockout then you've survived your attack.

Now here's the other thing.

I'm not going to suggest you join a boxing club in order to learn how to throw a punch.

You can, but I suspect you either already know how to throw a punch… or you don't,

And knowing how to throw a punch doesn't necessarily mean you can do it, or do it well, especially under pressure.

So there's no real 'in between' when it comes to this.

You either can (through varying degrees of effectiveness).

Or you can't.

And based on the fact that you've bought this book you clearly want to *know* how to defend yourself and not *learn* how to defend yourself.

And all through the medium of the written word as opposed to the sweaty boxing gym.

And I fully understand that, but I will give you one simple training drill so at least you can see for yourself whether or not you can actually throw a punch as I always thought it was easy to do a back flip until I tried doing one.

Stand in front of a mirror, with your hands raised up in a boxing style position (Google it if you don't know what that looks like) and send a punch using your most powerful hand straight out and back again as you would if you were doing it for real, in order to see what it looks like.

If it's all over the place then keep doing it until you can send it in a straight line, ideally from your chin or chest height to the target (which will be your attacker's jaw in this case).

Once you can do this then try doing it with your eyes closed.

Then get that ping pong ball out again and try hitting it.

Then try hitting it using only your middle knuckle.

Then with your eyes closed.

When you can do all of this your punch is probably ready.

….

The Solar Plexus
Now lots of people suggested you *kick* someone in the
SOLAR PLEXUS and they would be correct in suggesting
this, except for one small, minute, little, over looked
point….
Most people *can't* kick well enough to be able to pull one
off.

Unless you are an experienced kicker I'd suggest you keep
both of your feet firmly on the ground at all times.

Instead and only if the jaw isn't available, send that same
punch from above into your attacker's solar plexus with
everything you've got.

If you hit it right, they'll drop like a sack of spuds.

If not, then adapt the Tasmanian Devil persona one more
time.

If you decide to ignore my advice then kick using a front
(facing) kick only and be sure you have the right distance.

A kick is designed for long range fighting so if you try to
kick someone when you are actually standing in punching
range (close enough to punch them) you may well find that
your kick doesn't work.

A front kick to the body (solar plexus) is best done when
your attacker is heading towards you and you still have
room to kick.

Your kick combined with their forward movement may well double the impact and consequently the stopping power.

A rear leg kick will generate more power but don't worry too much about this.

Just use the same leg to kick with as you'd use to kick a football as far as you could.

As with your writing hand, this is the best way to determine which is the most powerful leg to use.

Lots or self defence experts will tell you to use a round kick, or a side kick, or a spinning back kick, but here's the thing again… they're all hard kicks to pull off if you're not used to doing them.

They require a certain degree of flexibility, combined with balance, body mechanics and know how.

You're obviously welcome to try but keep in the back of your mind, once again, that this isn't a movie and you're not Jason Statham.

Plus, I've seen people try to kick, get their leg grabbed and end up on the floor.

I remember an old girlfriend of mine coming to watch me compete once and she couldn't believe how scrappy the fighting was compared to the Karate Kid movie we had watched together.

Movies are choreographed, fights aren't.

Even Bruce Lee had to re-take the incredibly famous nunjaku scene in Enter the Dragon several times before he got it right.

The liver

To target the LIVER effectively you need to have one of several things in place.

One, your attacker's liver in easy, straight line reach of your most powerful hand, which will probably mean if you are right handed they need to be turned more round to the right when they engage you.

Two, be left handed (as that will probably be the hand nearest to your attacker's liver if they are standing directly in front of you).

If you're concerned about this then either don't worry about hitting the liver as worrying about it will cause you a problem under pressure.

Or start training up your left hand so that you *can* eventually send a powerful left handed straight punch (more work on your part though).

Know (or learn -- more work on your part) how to throw a left handed hooking punch.

Know (or learn -- more work on your part) how to deliver a crippling round kick to this area.

Or just don't worry about it.

Based on the awkwardness and close proximity requirement, I might suggest you simply don't worry about this area, especially given the fact that I'm not encouraging you to get too close to your attacker at this stage.

And of course completely rule out the body if your attacker is wearing a thick winter coat as the coat will probably absorb much of the energy of your body shot.

The Groin

Unless you leave your front door wide open all night, it's probably fair to say that should you find yourself unlucky enough to be confronted with an attacker, there's a higher percentage it's going to be outside of your home rather than in it.

And if it is inside your home then there's a good chance you will have some solid object around you that you can instantly use as a weapon (even a TV remote control can do masses of damage of you hit someone in the face with it).

Or you will have discovered them as you walk through the front door.

Or they bundle you into your home (which happens) as you open your front door.

And if it is outside in the street, or you're just entering your property then you should be wearing shoes of some description.

And those shoes should have a solid bit at the front that protects your toes.

So, I want you to imagine there's a football placed right underneath your attacker's **GROIN**.

You're going to swing your leg towards your attacker's groin, aiming to strike with the point of your shoes just like you would if you were going to toe poke a football as far as you could across a playing field.

Note of caution....

I'm assuming now that your footwear offers adequate toe protection.

If not, if you're wearing flip flops, or bare feet, or if there's any doubt that your shoes aren't all that strong then you should strike using the ball of the foot.

To do this pull your toes back as you kick.

You don't need to bend them right back so that they lay flat across your instep (as they won't), but just enough to get them out of the way initially.

As your foot connects with the target, the solidity of the target you are kicking will take care of pushing the toes back the rest of the way which in turn will pave the way for that solid bone, just at the base of the toes (the ball of the foot) to connect with the target instead.

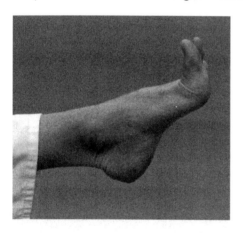

Do NOT kick with your toes if you have bare feet or flip flops as you'll likely break them on impact.

Try gently kicking the wall (low level) to see how bending your toes back and striking with the ball of your foot works.

If you have access to a hanging punch bag then you can practice the same thing by striking the bottom of the bag to simulate the groin.

Or get someone to hold something solid and practice striking that as you would the groin.

If you have solid shoes on you can use the instep to strike the groin with but take care with this.

Behind the groin is solid bone and although you may finish an attack with one good solid swift kick in this area, if you use the instep to strike with without much protection there's a risk of you injuring, if not breaking, your foot.

My suggestion therefore would be a good pair of solid shoes and a toe strike.

….

The Shin
I would suggest you kick the shin using the point of a solid shoe.

You *can* use the ball of the foot as described above but it won't be as effective and, as the only real reason you'd use the ball of your foot is because you had bare feet or inadequate protection, then due to the risk factor of you breaking a toe, I'd suggest you target another area instead.

It's easier for the toes to be pushed out of the way as your leg / foot is angled as it swings upwards towards the groin than it is when kicking a vertical target such as the shin.

The Foot

This is best attacked from very close range such as if you find yourself grabbed from either the front or behind.

Simply stamp down as hard as you can onto your attackers foot using your heel.

Pull your toes back as you stamp to ensure you use the smallest point of the heel to maximise the impact.

If you connect with the sole or arch of your foot you run the risk of dispersing the energy of the attack a little too much as you connect with a greater or softer surface area which could reduce the overall impact.

A smaller, harder striking area will cause maximum damage to a weak area such as the attacker's instep.

Again a solid pair of shoes will offer your heel maximum protection as you connect, especially if your attacker is also wearing a solid pair of shoes.

If you are barefoot or wearing softer shoes and find yourself grabbed or too close to punch then consider a head butt to their nose instead.

As mentioned before, a strike to the nose may not end an attack but it might just cause enough of a reaction in your attacker to provide you with enough distance to then punch or escape.

And don't worry about the head butt.

All you need to do is drive your forehead (if grabbed from the front), the top of your head (if grabbed from above), or the back of your head towards where you believe their nose is.

If it connects with any part of their face, you are going to get a reaction which might be enough to let you send a solid shot, or escape.

Building Your Wall

Building a good solid wall between you and your attacker will help you set up your pre-emptive strike, raise your defences, keep your attacker at bay and all without your attacker even knowing what you are doing.

As you know a wall is a solid object that protects your property.

You property in this case is you, and your wall is your stance and hand positioning.

When first faced with an attack you have several options.

You can become docile and consequently an easy target.

You can become aggressive and possibly find yourself with a bigger problem.

Or you can become assertive and take control of the situation.

As it's probably fair to assume that anyone approaching you looking to either fight, rob or attack you, is likely to be high on adrenaline and ready to go to war if they have to.

If you come back at them in any way that could be interpreted as hostile, you massively increase the chances of ending up in some kind of a fight.

Squaring up, puffing out your chest, raising your hands, clenching your fists are all aggressive signals and will be subconsciously interpreted by your attacker that you're going to fight back.

As a result, you may not necessarily get the first shot in and not doing so could cost you dearly.

Becoming docile will mean you may still get hurt as the attacker will realise you have no intention of fighting back so they can carry on regardless and with no worry about themselves getting hurt.

Becoming assertive means that you take control of yourself in the situation which will give you a greater chance of striking first and surviving the ordeal.

When initially confronted resist the temptation to rub noses with your attacker.

Instead take a step back and raise your open hands as shown below.

As you step back be sure to step back so that your dominant hand (the one you write with) is now at the back.

In the picture above you can see that it's the right hand (mirror image).

The left hand is slightly in front and consequently closer to the attacker.

The hands are held open which is a non aggressive pose, and they are positioned between you and your attacker.

If they were closed now the picture above would look much different.

And the facial expression is one of '*I don't want any trouble*'.

This is 'your wall'.

You have put a physical barrier between you and your attacker (your hands) and subconsciously your attacker will pick up on this although to them it will only look like you're doing the stereotypical and universally recognised '*I don't want to fight you*' pose.

As you're displaying all the signs of not being a threat, there's a good chance at this stage your attacker will come down slightly off their adrenaline high.

It's at this point that you would send your pre-emptive strike.

If you go for the eyes, your lead hand is already in position and you could probably take it closer still without your attacker realising it.

The closer you can get your lead hand to your attackers eyes before you strike, the greater the chance of you landing your attack.

Your rear (dominant) hand is set up ready for the big shot to the jaw.

Here you can could either just send it on its own, send the lead hand to the eyes and then send the rear hand to the jaw or, if they attempt to knock your lead hand out of the way because they feel it's too close to them, send the rear shot instantly.

You are also set up for your punch to the solar plexus.

Or your rear leg kick to the groin.

So as you can see, using 'the wall' has many advantages.

Not only is it submissive and not threatening in approach.

It also creates a natural barrier between you and your attacker.

And it puts your body into the perfect position to strike from.

Picture the guy in the photo above with clenched fists and you basically have the standard fighting stance.

In Summary

My intention with this book was to help anyone out there worried about what to do should they ever find themselves in a real life, street attack situation.

I wanted to keep the book short and sweet.

Not because I thought I'd just write as little as possible.

But because I have many books on my book shelves that I've just never read.

Mainly because there's just too much information in them.

And too much information isn't always necessary.

Or even a good thing.

In fact often, *too* much information is as bad as too little.

And most of it I don't really need to know about.

You don't need to know how an engine works in order to drive the car.

Just learn how to *drive* it.

And drive it.

And so I wanted you to be able to pick this up, read it in about an hour and from doing so understand a little bit more than you already do.

I've particularly aimed it at the individual that *doesn't* want to have to join a weekly martial arts class in order to put everything into practice.

None of the pre-emptive strikes are longer than one, solitary move.

They really couldn't be simpler.

And you can carry them all out without the need to spend hours pounding away on a heavy bag each week in order to develop your punching power.

Easy to remember.

And no further training required.

If you were intent on becoming the next cage fighting world champion then this is something completely different and training would be the *only* way.

However, you don't need to thrust your fingers into a bowl full of jelly ten thousand times in order to be able to thrust them into someone's eye socket should you ever need to do it for real.

You don't need to spend hours and hours kicking the base of a tree in order to be able to kick someone in the shin.

Your biggest challenge is actually '*doing it for real*' should you ever need to.

And you can't really train for that.

You can't spend hours poking your training partner in the eye just to see if you can do it and how they react when you do.

You can't spend hours kicking someone in the groin.

When I got attacked all those years ago I thought I might die and the memory of that attack has stayed with me forever.

,r to say it mentally scarred me.

d have had just a bit more information on what I *could*
ave done, it might have been enough to change the
outcome.

I got beaten up and put in hospital anyway.

And that happened because I did nothing.

It certainly couldn't have been any worse for me had I tried
fighting back.

Thinking '*I better not defend myself in case I annoy them*'
made no difference whatsoever.

Had I fought back, the outcome may well have been
different.

It may have been enough to cause them to flee.

A full on fight in the street *may* have encouraged someone
to step in and break it up.

It would certainly have attracted lots of attention and that's
not always a good thing for the street attacker.

I also don't want you to think I wrote this book purely to
make money.

It's my life's work and it's on sale for less than that pint of
beer or glass of wine that you'll buy from the one place you
may well get attacked in.

If you want to read more on the subject then I would highly
recommend anything from Geoff Thompson.

He in turn recommends his favourites.

But here's the thing.

Even if you do feel a little more confident.

Maybe now able to end an attack should it ever happen to you.

The biggest thing I want you to take away from this book is that it is possible with a little understanding and an ounce of common sense that you *never* actually find yourself in a situation where you *do* have to test it all out for real.

And never.

Ever.

EVER.

Take that short cut, across a dimly lit field… at night

Printed in Great Britain
by Amazon